Talking to Irwin

Talking to Irwin

Poems by

Lee Chottiner

Cover design by Shay Culligan
Cover image by Jon Tyson on Unsplash
Photo of Irwin Lee Moskowitz is a family photo; all rights are reserved
Author photo by Noa Chottiner

ISBN: 979-8-90146-604-9
Library of Congress Control Number: 2026931918

Kelsay Books
502 South 1040 East, A-119
American Fork, Utah 84003
Kelsaybooks.com

For Irwin Lee Moskowitz, my uncle for whom I am named, who died tragically in 1929 in Clairton, Pennsylvania, when he was 4. These poems are his unfinished story.

For all souls who left us before they truly lived.

And always for Beth and Noa,
my readers who matter most.

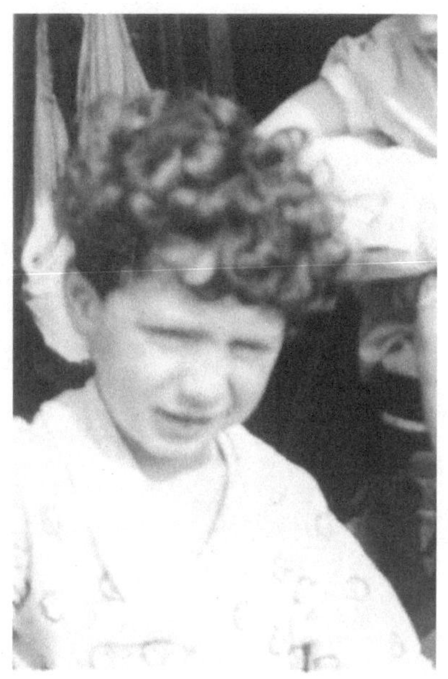

Irwin Lee Moskowitz

Acknowledgments

No book, not even this thin chapbook, comes to life with just the labor of the poet. So, I am grateful for some special people who helped me through the process. But for their keen eyes, literary sense, and moral support, my journey with Irwin might never have reached its destination.

First, I am grateful to Cheryl Moskowitz, a prominent American English poet and my first cousin, for providing some much-needed inspiration through her splendid poem, "Wilson Avenue," which also touched on Irwin's tragic death. Cheryl took my manuscript, read it carefully, then sat me down for an honest and thoughtful critique. This chapbook is more complete and telling because of her.

My good friend Bill Brymer, a prolific Kentucky poet and Pushcart Prize nominee, read the manuscript multiple times, coming to know Irwin almost as well as me. Bill offered tweaks to the manuscript where he thought they were needed, invariably improving the verses. He also showed me how a compliment can be just as instructive as a criticism.

Liz Prather—friend, teacher, and a gem of a Kentucky poet—also read the manuscript and urged me to not give up my search for a publisher. She believed, perhaps more than me, that there was a home for it.

This book would not be possible without the love, support, and understanding of my wife, Beth, and my daughter, Noa. They believed in me even when I found it difficult to do so. That day in a Pittsburgh cemetery, when they stood with me before Irwin's grave, becoming his family in a way far more lasting than blood or marriage, meant more to me than they will ever know.

Lastly, I thank you, the reader, for living with these poems, if only for a short time, helping to give Irwin the legacy that fate denied him. For that, I am in your debt.

Contents

Being named for a dead child is like living
for two souls, fearing the fate of both
when you, too, finally die.

i

Children, like seedlings
in need of nurturing, can
grow tall and bear fruit—
learning, loving, and living—
but comes the crash of the ax.

Blank Space

The job form on the screen
has a space for middle names,

my piece of name I have rarely
used, but now I see you standing

in that photo, your father's hand
resting on your tiny shoulder,

or maybe gripping it, holding
you back, but from what?

Maybe a violent moment
that the old man could see,

but you, so young, could not,
being 4, never to grow old.

You ran into that street and . . .

~

Your mother's hair
turned white overnight,

they say, so her doctor
prescribed another child,

a replacement life, to be
so blunt, who grew up,

had me, gave me your name
to wear like a tarnished ring.

Wear it I would, my
lifeless inheritance.

Wear it I would,
my ill-fitting name,

though growing up, learning
to write, losing jobs again

and again, your little name
grew old and cold and stiff.

~

Now, middle aged, my time
too grows brittle and stiff,

like the vanishing name,
easier to crumple and rip.

So, staring at that blank
space, I find you a place

to play where your name
may stay young and fresh.

Like your replacement,
I have nothing else to give

but my name, your name.
So, I fill the blank space in.

I type—I rewrite—Irwin.

I Don't Know How

to keep you alive.
I alone have your
name, making me
the banker of your
brief existence.
Your name, my vault,
for as long as I live.

I forgot that day
in the cemetery
where you lay,
as if I too killed
you, just as the
truck driver with
no time to brake.

I wandered the hill,
weaving my way
through granite
mazes, seeking
your grave, reading
etched names that
weren't yours.

I know I can’t
restore your life,
and I too must die.
So . . .
I have decided
that we must talk.
Pull up a planet and listen.

I Won't Talk About How You Died

I am 65, but the boy I
was heard grown-ups talk
only of how you died
and not a word more.

Funny, for I still don't know
for sure how it happened.
Maybe you chased a ball,
or an apple, rolling away.

I heard your brother held
your hand before the end.
Either he let go, or you did.
Time drops curtains like this.

But a "1927 Chevy pick-up
(best on the street!),"[1]
was the deadly weapon,
my cousin wrote in her poem;

I don't know if it's true,
I just know that the sum
of your little life equals
a deafening death.

---

[1] *From "Wilson Avenue" by Cheryl Moskowitz,* The Girl is Smiling *(Circle Time Press, Great Britain 2012).*

But once, while a boy,
my mother reminded me
that "the *yahrzeit* of your
Uncle Irwin" had arrived

that week—the only
time she called you
my uncle, why then
I will never know.

I only know how strange
it is to think of a 4-year-
old boy as an uncle, not
grown to a man of means.

I only know she never
had you for a brother.
She never tagged
after you to school

or told you, side eye
and winking, how her
girlfriend wished|
you would ask her out.

No brush strokes
on your canvass like
that, just choking sounds
a braking truck makes.

But I won't talk
about how you died,
I will talk about how
you might have lived,

how having your name,
is like wearing your
long-moldered skin.
Let the what-ifs begin.

The Truck Driver

He sees you through
his peripheral vision

rushing in front of
his grille—a flash

of life, then gone. An
accidental executioner,

he becomes withdrawn,
watered by whiskey

from that day on (or
so I imagine). I don't

know his name, but
maybe you have met

him, forgiven him.
So, I want to pause

to say how *I* forgive
him. Let's move on.

Lids and Pots

What would you do
and who would you marry?
Questions, like lives, can die.

. . .

Grandma said, "There's a lid for every pot."
Did she mean yours was already cast?
Did a lid (or pot) wait for you?

. . .
. . .
. . .

Did it die waiting?
. . .

Perhaps pantries exist
where you are,
shelves stocked with missing lids and pots
waiting to be filled
by stews never cooked.

. . .
. . .

Is that where you are?
. . .
. . .

What becomes of untasted love?
Ashes, perhaps, escaping smokestacks
long since torn down in your hometown.

. . .

No.
Your love must still be here,
drenching the dirt
like heavy rain,
keeping the country green.

Curls

I bet your mother ran her fingers
through your harvest of hair,
something you would never do,
too young for a child of your own
when you left here all alone.

But I have a daughter whose hair
curls gently like yours. I see her
quietly decoding her homework
at night, finally calling me to see
how she plotted points on a graph.

I puzzle through all those pencil
points freckling four quadrants
without fail, table after table she
completes, and solutions too—
y=-2x + 3 when x=-2.

You'd be proud of her perfect scores,
the many math mysteries she solves,
and those curls draping her face
as she searches mine for love.
You too might have plotted points,

I have thought, had you stayed,
searching another face for love.
Or maybe not, I don't know,
having just snapshots of you
to go on, which isn't enough.

To Be Honest . . .

No one told me
to live my life for you,
to build a house for two
with blueprints of future,
to never be blind
to your oblivion,
to find a legacy for you.

No one described you
to me; no one sat me down,
telling me how you used
to frown at the clingy sound
your toy truck made
as you sat on the rug,
racing it through the fibers.

Even your parents hoarded
tidbits of the boy they knew,
never saying how your voice
sounded, if you picked pears
from their tree in the back.
Whatever they knew of you,
they took away with them.

I want to sip life with you,
grapes from our two vines
crushed and casked for a wine
with grave-tasting tannins,
but that heady beverage takes
two whole lives to ferment.
Our vintage is left unfinished.

White Shroud

Her shock of white hair
looked pure, like a shroud,
mourning for her red hair,
which packed its bags

long ago and left town,
anxious to be wherever
you might be. That was
all she wanted, I think.

They say her red hair
looked stunning, turning
men's heads at the corner
of St. Clair and Miller.

But I only saw the white,
which seemed like snow
on a roof, keeping her attic
below full of heirlooms

silent and warm. That's
where I like to think you
went, waiting for her,
sleeping in her quilt of red.

So, are you together now?
Did she ever reclaim all
that lustrous red? Is she as
young as you remember?

And what shade of red?
I don’t even know if it
was a dusky auburn or
an old-world ginger.

Little things like that
I wish I could know,
but I can’t. You see,
I only have you to ask.

Heaven

Once
Only once
did she
speak
of you
to me

Sitting
in her
Pittsburgh
apartment
not far
from the
rest home
where she
would lose
her mind
she told
me that
you were
in Heaven
&
knew who
she was

I don't
know what
Heaven
looks like
(maybe
like the
planet
on which
you now
sit)
but she
held that
bit of
you to
the end

That was
all she
shared
of you
with me
The rest
she left
blank
as if

daring me
to write
this now

After all
how far
am I
from my
own rest
home where
I too
will lose
my mind

ii

Dead too young to live,
you never knew your sister,
and she would not know
you, but just like me I see
that she never escaped you.

She, the Replacement

How

do you go

through

life

as a spare

part

a heart

that is yours

but

little

else

and you know

you are here

only because

he

is

. . . *not*

I'd Like to Meet the Doctor

I'd like to meet the doctor
who told your father
how your grieving mother
needed another child
to replace the one she lost.

I'd like to ask the doctor
who told your father
to fill his prescription for
new life what words he
used to convince him.

I'd like to see the doctor
who told your father
this, give him a name,
draw him a face, filling
the space that he left.

I'd like to thank the doctor
who told your father
all he ought to do
to soften the sorrow borne
by his damaged wife.

The Price to Pay

She grew up as
an anticlimax
to your story,
which was told
with remnants
and threads.
What else was
there? No toys
from your chest,
no baseball from
your mitt.

She knew well
growing up
why she was
alive in your house
when she heard
her mother say
how a son was
her price to pay
for the daughter
she always wanted.

I Never Asked

She could have talked to you too,
and maybe she did. I never asked.

Sitting alone upstairs in her room,
her mom downstairs cooking cabbage,
her dad in the den smoking cigars,

she may have spent nights in bed
writing letters to you in her journal,
if she kept one. I never asked.

Being a dancer, she may have
spoken to you through movement—
a kick, a sway—hard to say what

way she had to ask how you were,
where you were, if she asked at all.
I don't know; I never asked.

She traveled chaotic trails with me—
fearful, phobic, violent miles—leaving
welts on my arms when my homework

proved too hard. She simply lacked
the patience to teach, though she tried.
I don't know why; I never asked.

Her pain became mine, making for
minefields of moments now, buried
questions I never dared to unearth.

She knew before me that we were
here because you were not, which
may explain the scars left behind.

I'll never know; I never asked.

iii

I still catch his gaze,
as he stays in his Kodak
cage while I am free.
Here I am, living for him
poeming a peace just for me.

The Inside-Out Name

What's in a name? That which we call a rose,
by any other name would smell as sweet.
—William Shakespeare

It feels at times
I wear my name
(or your name)
the wrong way

as a boy of 4
too young to know
the shirt tag goes
inside not out

Irwin Lee
Lee Irwin

Which is which
Who is who

Not my fault
The name was
handed to me
inside out

to spare your
mother the
nightmare that
whitened her hair

She is gone now
Only the twisted
name remains

and the boy
and the man
in a room
each gripping an end

figuring out
just how
the damn thing
should fit

I'd Like You to Meet . . .

Rosa
Rosa Levy
Born 1889
Died 1890

She lives in a grave
not far from your own

her headstone small
like a teddy bear

I found her one day
sleeping by the fence

while clearing the
grounds around her

She seemed lonely
so I pulled away

the twigs and vines
covering her little

space and left my
calling card pebble

I came back
another day

after vandals
defiled the space

spent condoms
raping the grass

stone homes
toppled and tired

Who does that
to a baby who died

without giggling
with girls at school

Thinking her lonely
I return to her grave

time after time after
time in my mind

writing her poems
I'll let you read them sometime

Anyhow . . .

I thought you might
keep her company

wherever you are
Even if she knows

folks on your side
it’s not like she

can talk to them
(toddlers rarely can)

So maybe you can
just hold her hand

make her understand
that you too know

something of leaving
a life barely lived

My Worst Fear

Do you not know that a man is not dead while his name is still spoken?
—Terry Pratchett

But you weren't a man,
you were barely a boy,
and imaginations *do* die.

Memories thin and dim
with time, and I forget
where I placed my wallet.

Do you want to know
my worst fear?
I will be old, lying

in a rest home bed,
eyes closed, lips stilled,
soiled until someone cleans me.

And you will be there
in that bed with me . . .
waiting, just waiting.

My father went that way,
his eyes still open
when I sat by his side

showing him his school
photos, but he just
couldn't find himself.

I might lose you that way
when my bedtime comes.
After all, we never met.

Bequeathed Immortality

When I die,
don't die with me,
whatever's left of you
riding the wind
from your mill town,
never to return.
I don't need
that kind of end.
You have become
my pen pal
sans ink.
In missives
to you I include
all things boys
ought to do
without fear
of losing a life:
hitting a ball,
swimming a pool,
punching a bully,
kissing a girl
(or a boy).
All this flesh
I want to graft
to your tiny soul.

Wear it like
a suit of clothes
wherever you go,
breathing fresh sighs
that take flight,
keeping your name
alive.

Resolution

I run this race
Sneakers laced
I pace myself
through rain-
soaked streets
stopping at
water stations
to hydrate
cooling down
moving on

You run too
you know
(no choice)
finishing
when I finish
Dying when I die   again
headstones alone
to show we
ever ran
the race at all

This is resolution
realization
I cannot raise the dead

I can’t step
before the truck
taking the hit
like a cosmic
bodyguard
surfing time
I’m not even
sure I’d want to
if saving you
meant losing me

The race must end

This is resolution
realization
I cannot raise the dead

One-Sided

I talked
You did not

You didn't even listen

Lost in the rooms
of the mansion

the ballroom piano
no longer played

You didn't even listen

I wanted you
to hear me

but knowing
you would not

Reality is a cold stew

So too the talk
grows cold

when just one voice
is heard

Olly Olly Oxen Free

You played Hide and Go Seek
with me when I
last came to visit.

I trudged up that hill
and down, checking
under every stone,

peeking in all
your hiding places.
I couldn't find you.

I found your mom and dad,
even your granddad,
but they were older
and not so keen on
playing games.

But you! You hid so well.

I played the game
for the longest time,
despairing of finding
you, fearing I failed you,

feeling I failed your sister
who cheated at the game
long ago by showing me
where you like to hide.

She knew one day
she too would go away
to hide. Someone
had to seek. Game on.

So, there I stood alone,
game lost, then my daughter
—your great-niece—shouted,
"Olly olly oxen free!"

(Really, she shouted your name,
"Irwin Lee Moskowitz!"
I came running all the same.
You were found.
Olly olly oxen free!)

And the prize for winning?
Getting to touch
your stony face,
which must be enough.
Game over.

About the Author

Lee Chottiner believes poetry is the people's voice—even if they don't always agree. A poet and newspaper reporter for more than 30 years, Lee's work has been published in several newspapers and journals, both here and abroad. *Talking to Irwin* is his first chapbook. Lee lives in Louisville, Kentucky, with his wife, Beth, his daughter, Noa, and his basset hound, Schenley.

www.ingramcontent.com/pod-product-compliance
Lightning Source LLC
LaVergne TN
LVHW090618110826
845146LV00001B/440

* 9 7 9 8 9 0 1 4 6 6 0 4 9 *